BUS DEALERS AND BREAKERS OF YORKSHIRE

KEITH A. JENKINSON

AMBERLEY

First published 2018

Amberley Publishing
The Hill, Stroud
Gloucestershire, GL5 4EP

www.amberley-books.com

Copyright © Keith A. Jenkinson, 2018

The right of Keith A. Jenkinson to be identified
as the Author of this work has been asserted
in accordance with the Copyright, Designs and
Patents Act 1988.

ISBN 978 1 4456 7492 6 (print)
ISBN 978 1 4456 7493 3 (ebook)

British Library Cataloguing in Publication Data.
A catalogue record for this book is available from
the British Library.

Origination by Amberley Publishing.
Printed in the UK.

Introduction

The county of Yorkshire has a long history in relation to the bus and coach industry, having had a wide range of manufacturers, dealers and dismantlers located within its boundaries, a number of which are still active today. Thus, a sizeable number of large passenger vehicles have remained in the county from cradle to grave, having, for example, being built by Plaxton, Roe or Optare, operated by a Yorkshire company, passed through one of the county's dealers and ended their life in one of the Barnsley area scrapyards.

My interest in bus dealers and breakers began in the early part of the 1950s with visits to W. North at Stourton, although a lack of courage stopped me from asking if I could enter the yard, meaning that I had to view its contents through the surrounding fence. After the company moved to Sherburn-in-Elmet, however, I was granted access to their new site and became a frequent visitor throughout the years; at least until W. North ceased trading in 2000. Meanwhile, in the early 1990s I began to visit the various breakers at Carlton, many of which became close friends, and without whom it would not have been possible to produce this book. To all those concerned, I am extremely grateful.

While most of the photographs are my own, I have used a number from other enthusiasts to enable full coverage of the subject, and to all those who have assisted me I offer them my grateful thanks, and sincerely apologise to those who I have been unable to credit due to a lack of knowledge as to their identity.

Keith A. Jenkinson
Queensbury, August 2017

Dealers

Yorkshire has for many years provided a home for new and second-hand bus and coach dealers. Among the earliest of these was Leeds-based Samuel Ledgard, who, in addition to his numerous and diverse business interests, including haulage and passenger transport, obtained the agency for the distribution of Caledon vehicles in 1918. This he continued until 1921, when he relinquished it and in its place took up the agency for American automobile company Pierce Arrow – although due to lack of sales this was terminated after only twelve months.

Next to venture into the new and used bus and coach market was J. W. Hall, at Huddersfield, who in the mid-1920s quickly became the largest company in its field in the north of England. However, concentrating solely on the resale market, any time-expired vehicles that Hall took in part exchange for more youthful vehicles were sold to Thomas Allsop of Sheffield for scrapping, as will be seen later. Following this, L. W. Elvins set up a business under the title W. North at Percy Street, Hull, in 1931, from where he too began selling second-hand buses and coaches. However, finding that Humberside was perhaps geographically unsuited for expanding his activities, he set about seeking a more central location, and in 1934 purchased some land at Whinmoor, some 6 miles from Leeds on the main York road. As a small stone-built workshop and several tiny outbuildings already occupied this site, these provided him with an amount of space for the storage of vehicle spares, as well as giving him a workshop in which maintenance could be undertaken. Meanwhile, James Stanley Kaye had set up a business in Leeds in 1921, selling second-hand cars and motorcycles and motor spares from a small site in St Pauls Street in the city centre. Later, he moved to larger premises on Holme Street off South Accommodation Road, before relocating once more to a plot of land on Pontefract Road, Stourton. Having added second-hand buses and coaches to his portfolio in 1937, and wishing to expand in this field, he suggested to L. W. Elvins in 1938 that they should merge their businesses under the W. North name, and to this end a large plot of land was found further along Pontefract Road to work from. With Elvins no longer needing his Whinmoor site, this was sold to J. S. Kaye for use in connection with his car spares business, while as a consequence of the outbreak of the Second World War, Huddersfield-based J. W. Hall ceased trading.

Prior to these events, another second-hand bus and coach dealer appeared on the scene when P. M. Morrell set up in business on Hunslet Road, Leeds, in the mid-1930s. Although he additionally began dismantling time-expired vehicles, with the sales side of his business gaining momentum he entered into an agreement with Thomas Allsop to undertake his scrapping activities. After the latter took the decision to retire in 1939,

Morrell purchased his business and continued this at Hunslet Road until he himself retired in 1955.

Following the return to peace in 1945, W. North began to grow rapidly to become Britain's largest second-hand bus and coach dealer. In 1952, W. North entered into a contract with London Transport to purchase around 1,300 of its surplus buses, which under a restriction placed on them by London could only be sold to overseas customers or for non-PSV use in the UK (except in approved circumstances). In the event, however, W. North negotiated an amendment to this ruling, allowing them to sell up to 10 per cent of these vehicles to home market operators.

Meanwhile, in order to assist the company with its overseas sales, it set up an office at London Transport's Chiswick works as a point of convenience for foreign customers (who could view some of the buses on offer without having to visit Leeds). This resulted in a large number of the buses that were exported never making the 200-mile northbound journey, instead being driven directly from London to the docks at Dover, from where they were shipped mainly to Ostend or Dunkirk before travelling much further afield. In December 1962, W. North vacated its Stourton site to make way for a new railway freight terminal, relocating to a large new base at Sherburn-in-Elmet, from where it continued its second-hand bus and coach sales and rentals. In addition, although it undertook a small amount of dismantling at both Stourton and its new site, it largely sold its non-resaleable vehicles to other dismantlers, as will be seen, before finally taking the decision to cease trading in 2000, selling all its remaining stock and sundry equipment to Carlton-based Trevor Wigley.

Entering the passenger vehicle market in 1951, selling new and second-hand coaches, was Stanley Hughes at Gomersal, midway between Leeds and Bradford. After growing in strength, the company was ultimately purchased in 1982 by the Barnsley-based Paul Sykes Group, who gained the UK dealership for DAF and Van Hool buses and coaches before selling the business in 1988 to Tom Cowie PLC, who rebranded it as Arriva Bus & Coach in 1997. Although Arriva was acquired by the German transport giant Deutsche Bahn in 2010, the sales and service arm continues to trade today without a change of direction or title. While under Paul Sykes's ownership, new vehicles were often stored at his Barnsley premises due to restricted space at the Gomersal site. Today, the Barnsley premises serve as Stagecoach Yorkshire's depot. Not far away from Stanley Hughes was Cleckheaton-based Jack Hughes, who also dealt in new and second-hand coaches for three decades.

Another company in Yorkshire to become involved in second-hand bus and coach sales was Comberhill Motors of Wakefield, which was largely a lorry distributor and dealer. In the early part of the 1950s, however, the company extended its activities to purchasing small-capacity passenger vehicles, such as Bedford OWBs and OBs, Commer Commandos and Austin CXBs, mainly for sale to overseas customers – particularly those in Cyprus and Ceylon (before it was renamed Sri Lanka). Additionally, it also bought a few larger-capacity buses, such as Bristol L5Gs, for export to Macau, and ex-London Transport Guy Arabs and AEC Regal Is for export to Ceylon, Southern Rhodesia and the Canary Islands. Although it continued its used passenger vehicle activities into the mid-1960s, it then returned to its roots within the lorry market.

Paul Sykes (who is mentioned earlier and will crop up again later) began his transport-related activities as a bus dismantler at Blacker Hill Sidings on the outskirts of Barnsley in 1961 before gradually diversifying into selling used buses and coaches in the 1970s, as well as continuing to scrap them. Then, in 1978, he moved his sales activities to a new site on Barnsley Road, Athersley, before moving to larger premises across the road. A large part of his relocated business was concentrated on the overseas market with the sale of engines and mechanical units, in addition to complete buses, and this continued until he left the industry completely in 1988.

Similarly, Allan Finlay, who also traded as Hartwood Exports (Machinery) Ltd from premises at Birdwell, on the fringe of Barnsley, had also started as a dismantler, but soon changed direction to become an exporter, largely of engines and other mechanical units, but occasionally of complete buses too. Among the latter were forty-four ex-London Transport AEC Merlins, which he sold to Mauritius in 1977. However, some of these were only ever used for spares to support those employed in service.

Another dealership set up by bus breakers was that formed jointly by Carlton-based PVS and Trevor Wigley in 1992. For the new business, former bus and coach operator Arthur Rowe's depot at Cudworth (a mile or so from Carlton) was purchased, and it was here that the buses and coaches that both companies deemed were too good to scrap, and which could be resold for further use, were stored. In addition, this site was occasionally used as a place to store vehicles awaiting scrapping when their Carlton yards were filled to their limit. The business was, however, closed in 2004, after which the Cudworth site was sold for a housing development. Since 2008, Wigley again began selling buses for further use – albeit only in small quantities – from his Boulder Bridge Lane yard, and continues thus today.

In the meantime, while remaining largely as dismantlers at Boulder Bridge Lane, Carlton, Joe Sykes, Alan Hardwick and Geoff Ripley all undertook a small amount of dealing and sold buses for further PSV use, with the latter two still doing so today.

Further south at Hellaby on the fringe of Rotherham was bus and coach dealer Stuart Johnson, who from January 1975 traded as Carlton PSV Ltd. In addition to selling second-hand buses and coaches, the company took on the dealership for Neoplan, and in January 2000 changed its name to Neoplan UK Ltd and continued in business until June 2009. In the meantime, Carlton PSV had also moved into bus operation with the purchase (under the ATL banner) of National Travel (East), part of Crosville and Yelloways of Rochdale in 1988, and had begun operations around Sheffield and Leeds as SUT, which survived for only a few years before disappearing from the scene. Following the departure of Carlton PSV/Neoplan UK, Dawsonrental opened a rental/ sales site at Hellaby, which is still active today.

More recently, bus and coach manufacturer Plaxton of Scarborough set up a new and used sales arm at North Anston, near Sheffield, which concentrates its resale activities on new vehicles and those acquired through part-exchange deals. Similarly, bus manufacturer Optare of Sherburn-in-Elmet has also begun to undertake the occasional resale of vehicles obtained in part-exchange for new ones from its site in Carrington, on the outskirts of Manchester.

This view of James Stanley Kaye's original yard at St Paul's Street, Leeds, in around 1923 shows a potential customer examining various vehicles, including Model T Fords in the process of being dismantled. (W. North (PV) Ltd)

This poor-quality photograph shows W. North's Stourton yard in September 1961, with ex-Yorkshire Traction, Roe-rebodied Guy Arab II HE 9788, former West Yorkshire Road Car Co. ECW-bodied Bristol L5G DWW 576 and an unidentified ex-Mansfield District double-decker.

Standing among other double-deckers in North's Stourton yard in 1950 is former Barrow Corporation Massey-bodied wartime Daimler CWG5 92 (EO 7905).

100 DOUBLE DECK
BUSES 56 SEATERS by
LEYLAND and GUY

Guys manufactured in 1943/4/5, fitted with 5LW Gardner Diesel Engines are for Export only. Certificate of fitness for 3 years. **£450**

Leyland TD5 56 seaters, certified for 2 years, 8.6 Diesel Engines, crash gearboxes. All maintained to a very high standard. **£450**

All makes of Chassis fitted 5LW Gardner Diesel Engines for haulage from **£375**

Leyland Chassis only fitted 8.6 Diesels, Bristols, A.E.C., Daimlers— all makes and spares in stock. **£275**

EXPERT EXAMINATION WELCOMED.

Telephone: 23482 and 26248.
Telegrams: BUSNORTH, LEEDS.

W. NORTH of LEEDS LTD., 94, VICAR LANE, LEEDS, ENGLAND.

One of W. North's many early 1950s trade adverts; this one shows an ex-London Transport wartime Guy Arab along with details of other buses being offered for sale. (W. North (PV) Ltd)

Pictured outside W. North's Stourton yard in 1953 in the hope of finding an owner is former London Transport underfloor-engined Leyland Tiger TF27 (FJJ 638). (W. North (PV) Ltd)

Also photographed outside W. North's Stourton premises, albeit this time in 1954, is ex-United ECOC-bodied Bristol JO5G BJ31 (BHN 227), which quickly found a new owner and survived into the 1960s, latterly with a fairground showman. (W. North (PV) Ltd)

This aerial view of W. North's Whinmoor yard, taken around 1961, shows a wide variety of buses and small commercial vehicles awaiting their fate. In the foreground is the A64 Leeds to York road and on the left is the railway line. (W. North (PV) Ltd)

Standing 30 feet in the air at the front of W. North's Sherburn-in-Elmet premises for several years until the local council forced its removal was ex-Durham District ECW-bodied Bristol L5G DB171 (GHN 957), whose engine and running units had all been removed. (W. North (PV) Ltd)

Seen from the air is W. North's Sherburn-in-Elmet premises, with buses and coaches parked all around the hanger. Those vehicles outside the yard (on the extreme right) are awaiting collection by various breakers. (W. North (PV) Ltd)

Hopeful of finding buyers at W. North's Sherburn-in-Elmet yard in 1965 are a trio of open top ECW-bodied pre-war Bristol K5Gs: ex-Southern National 3824 (FHT 114); former Brighton, Hove & District 994 (EHY 581); and another unidentified ex-Brighton, Hove example.

For sale at W. North, Sherburn-in-Elmet, in September 1970, ex-Cheltenham & District Bristol KSW6B 85 (OHY 955) hides former Bristol Omnibus Co. Bristol KSW C8110 (OHY 967). Alongside it is ex-Western National Bristol KS5G 1806 (LTA825) and in the background is a former London Transport Leyland RTW.

Offered for sale at W. North's Sherburn-in-Elmet base in the autumn of 1966 are ex-Lancashire United NCME-bodied Guy Arab III 426 (MTB 52), former East Kent lowbridge Park Royal-bodied Guy Arab III EFN 189 and Harrington-bodied AEC Regal IV NTC 725, which began life with Liverpool coach operator Kenilworth.

Awaiting buyers at W. North, Sherburn-in-Elmet, in June 1966 are ex-West Yorkshire outrigged 8-foot-wide ECW-bodied Bristol LL5G SGW8 (JYG 723), former East Kent, Park Royal-bodied Guy Arab III EFN 175, Lancashire United NCME-bodied Foden PVD6s 450/49 (NTC 246/5) and ex-Rhondda, Weymann-bodied AEC Regent III 276 (MNY 537).

Seen at W. North's Sherburn-in-Elmet premises in 1965 are ex-Rotherham Corporation East Lancs (Bridlington)-bodied Bristol L5Gs 116/9 (FET 816/9) and ex-West Yorkshire ECW-bodied Bristol LWL6B JYG 746, which was originally registered JYG 741.

Seen together with some ex-Bristol Omnibus Co. Lodekkas at W. North's Sherburn-in-Elmet yard in 1981, and looking somewhat worse for wear, is prototype ECW-bodied Bristol LSX5G NHU 2, which began life as Bristol Omnibus Co. 2800 in 1950 and is now preserved.

Used for fourteen years by W. North (PV) Ltd in its hire fleet, ex-Bristol Omnibus Co. open top Bristol LD6G WHY 947 is seen here stored in the hanger at Sherburn-in-Elmet in 1982, together with North's preserved Leyland fire engine. The Lodekka was later sold to a preservationist in Holland. (Barry Newsome)

New to Standerwick, and later used by Tyne & Wear PTE, ECW-bodied Bristol VRLLH OCK 66K is seen here at W. North's Sherburn-in-Elmet premises in 1983, shortly before being exported to Australia. (Barry Newsome)

Starting life with Glasgow Corporation, Alexander-bodied Leyland PDR1A/1 (XGA 15J) had a number of owners before ultimately being acquired for preservation. It is seen here at W. North, Sherburn-in-Elmet, in June 1983 after being purchased from Dalehill Coaches, Doncaster.

One of a number of buses purchased by W. North from Holland for resale or spares, ex-VAD, Dusseldorp Verheul-bodied Leyland 2422 (Z-27-29) is seen in the yard at Sherburn-in-Elmet. (Barry Newsome)

A view of W. North's Sherburn-in-Elmet premises with buses from numerous operators, including Devon General, Ribble, Rhondda, Hebble, Bristol Omnibus Co. and Lancashire United.

Another view of W. North's Sherburn-in-Elmet yard, this time in June 1983, showing a selection of its large stock for resale or breaking.

Ex-Ribble NCME-bodied Leyland Atlantean 1951 (ECK9 51E), former Strathclyde PTE, Alexander-bodied Leyland Atlantean LA937 (JUS 784N) and ex-Grampian Regional Transport, Alexander-bodied Daimler CRG6LXs 134 (PRG 134J) and 132 (PRG 132J) stand together in W. North's Sherburn-in-Elmet yard in 1982. All except the ex-Ribble bus soon found new PSV owners.

After having been used by building contractors, Whitson-bodied Foden PVRF6 KWU 24, seen here in July 1985 at W. North's Sherburn-in-Elmet yard, fortunately found a buyer, saving it from the scrap man's torch.

Marshall-bodied Leyland Leopard UCK 544 began life as a bus with Ribble and was later converted to a horsebox, as seen here for sale at W. North, Sherburn-in-Elmet. It stands alongside former Western SMT, NCME-bodied Daimler CRG6LX GCS 161E, which latterly served with Paisley Hospital Radio.

Three of the buses used by W. North (PV) Ltd in its hire fleet: ex-National Travel (North West), Duple-bodied Leyland Leopards TTF 226/13M sandwich ex-Western SMT Alexander-bodied Leyland Leopard RSD 738J in the company's Sherburn-in-Elmet yard. (Author's collection)

Awaiting sale outside Arriva Bus & Coach at Gomersal on 17 February 2008 are ex-Classic, Annfield Plain, Irizar-bodied Scania K114IB4 YN53 OYX and former Sanders of Holt, Northern Counties-bodied DAF DB250 P336 ROO, which was new to Harris Bus, West Thurrock.

Standing outside Arriva Bus & Coach at Gomersal on 2 January 2010 are a brand new, and as yet unregistered, Arriva North East Temsa Avenue and ex-Gain Travel of Wibsey, Bradford's Van Hool T915 YJ08 EEX.

Ex-West Yorkshire Road Car Co., ECW-bodied Bristol L5G SG43 (CWY 981) heads through Leeds on trade plates en route to dealers Comberhill Motors, Wakefield, on 3 August 1956. It was quickly resold for a continued life in Macau. (Robert F. Mack)

Having been acquired in the 1950s from Comberhill Motors, Wakefield, by Lefkaritis, Larnaca, Cyprus, two Beadle-bodied Bedford OBs are seen withdrawn in their new owner's yard in October 1968.

Awaiting sale in Paul Sykes's Barnsley Road yard in August 1979 is an interesting selection of buses, among which are former Southdown Leyland PD3 Queen Marys, ex-Trent and Midland Red Daimler Fleetlines and an ex-Burnley & Pendle Bristol VRT.

Hellaby-based dealer Carlton PSV was also the agent for Neoplan. Here, new Neoplan Skyliner H201 AOD is seen in October 1990 at a trade exhibition at Telford immediately prior to its delivery to Trathens of Yelverton.

Ex-Southern Vectis Duple-bodied Bedford SB8 XDL 731 stands in the yard of Joe Sykes, Barnsley, in the vain hope of finding a buyer in November 1984.

For sale at Joe Sykes, Carlton, are ex-Armstrong, Westerhope, Alexander-bodied Seddon Pennine 7 RCS 708R, which was new to Western SMT, Willowbrook-bodied Bedford YMT LGR 51T and ex-Lothian Buses Seddon Pennine 4 CFS 108L.

Standing in Joe Sykes's Carlton yard in October 1986, and hopeful of finding a buyer, is ex-Merthyr Tydfil East Lancs-bodied Leyland Leopard 159 (EHB 259G), which is wearing the livery it had been painted into to commemorate the undertaking's 60th anniversary.

Although Rollinson was primarily a dismantler, a small number of the buses that entered his yard at Carlton were fortunate enough to find a buyer for continued use. One such bus was Bristol FS6G Lodekka 4225 FM, which had been new to Crosville but was acquired from Stafford Transport Training in October 1985. It was quickly sold to Clydeside Scottish for further driver training duties.

A trio of former Eastern Scottish driver trainers snuggle together in Wigley's Boulder Bridge Lane yard in April 1988. MCCW-bodied Leyland PD2 (JRJ 268E), which was new to Salford City Transport, was sold to a company in Belgium. It later found a new owner in Ireland in 2009 and was converted to semi-open top. Meanwhile, Bristol FLF6G (CSG 28C) was exported to Italy. The FLF6G in the centre was less fortunate, however, and was sadly scrapped.

Hopeful of finding buyers at the Cudworth yard of the joint PVS-Wigley dealership on 7 July 1995 are two Routemasters – ex-East Yorkshire LDS 337A (ex-WLT 364), which was ultimately sold to an owner in Poland, and former White Rose of Glasshoughton SVS 618 (ex-WLT 548), which gained a new home in the UK – and ex-Lincolnshire Road Car ECW-bodied Bristol LH6L 1052 (SVL 837R), which was not so lucky and soon became a pile of twisted metal at Boulder Bridge Lane.

Seen at the joint PVS-Wigley dealership at Cudworth, former Stagecoach United Counties Routemasters HVS 710 (ex-WLT 512) and ABD 892A (ex-68 CLT) await their departure in August 1999 to a new life in Mexico.

Having failed to find buyers, ex-Leon, Finningley NCME-bodied Leyland AN68 RJA 703R and former First Calderline NCME-bodied Leyland FE30AGR BVR 70T, both of which began life with Greater Manchester PTE, are seen here at PVS-Wigley's Cudworth site on 18 February 2002, awaiting removal for scrapping at Boulder Bridge Lane.

Seen leaving PVS's Boulder Bridge Lane yard for its short journey to the Cudworth sales site on 27 October 2001 is much-travelled ex-London Routemaster RM2210 (CUV 210C), which served with Clydeside Scottish, East Yorkshire, who converted it to open top, and then MacTours, Edinburgh, before crossing the water to Toronto, Canada, in 2009.

Offered for sale by Wigley at its Boulder Bridge Lane site on 6 March 2007 are ex-Stagecoach Wales Plaxton-rebodied Dennis Dart 32997 (K97 XNY) and Arriva North East Leyland Lynx 5011 (J651 UHN), neither of which succeeded in finding new owners, being subsequently scrapped.

Ex-Blackburn ECW-bodied Leyland Olympian 85 (D145 FYM), former Ellie Rose, Hull, East Lancs-bodied Dennis Facon H YDX 195Y and ex-Imperial, Romford, MCW Metrobus E455 SON are offered for sale at Wigley's Boulder Bridge Lane yard on 28 February 2008, although only the single-decker was ultimately sold.

Awaiting sale at Plaxton's, Hellaby, in May 2017 is former Compass Bus, Durrington, Stagecoach-liveried Alexander Dennis Enviro200 MX58 VGR, which was new to Bu-Val, Smithybridge. In the background a number of coaches, all seeking new owners, can be seen. (Plaxton).

Seen in 2013 while offered for rental, lease or sale by Dawsonrentals is former First CentreWest Mercedes-Benz 0530G bendibus 11018 (LK53 FBU).

Breakers

Bus dismantling in Yorkshire began in 1926, when Thomas Allsop began his activities in this field at Worthing Road, Attercliffe, Sheffield, as mentioned earlier. A large part of his stock was acquired from Huddersfield-based bus and coach dealer J. W. Hall, and as his business grew, he relocated to a larger site at Woodsetts Aerodrome, to the south of Sheffield, in 1933. In the meantime, the aforementioned J. S. Kaye began scrapping buses at Pontefract Road, Stourton, as too did dealers W. North and P. M. Morrell, albeit in a comparatively small way – mainly to provide a source of spares for the buses they sold. Although there were other breakers in the Leeds and Bradford area, such as C. E. Houghton and C. Waugh at Leeds and John Hornby at Bradford, these were small and concentrated largely on the scrapping of cars and lorries and so on, as too did Norman Blamires, who began his activities from a small, cramped yard at St Dunstans, close to Bradford city centre, in the mid-1930s. From the early 1950s, however, Blamires began to concentrate more on buses and coaches, and in 1964 was joined by his stepson, Brian Jackson, who took over the business following his stepfather's death in December 1965, continuing until 1970, when he left the industry and closed the yard.

Meanwhile, G. W. Butler, a general scrap merchant who had set up in business in 1933 at Bowling Iron Works, Bradford, briefly turned his attention to bus breaking in 1952 when, following the death of his friend – independent bus operator Samuel Ledgard – he purchased all the vehicles that had been stored on the roof of the latter's Armley depot since their withdrawal several decades earlier and quickly reduced these to piles of tangled metal. Included among these were steam wagons and charabancs that had been taken out of service in the 1920s, and it was a shame that the preservation movement had not yet begun in the early 1950s, as these would have undoubtedly been quickly snapped up and restored. In addition to his premises in Bradford, G. W. Butler also had a small yard near his home at Eller Ghyll, Menston, where a few more ex-Ledgard buses were scrapped until 1959, after which he returned to his general metals roots. Another breaker to be found in the Bradford area was run by brothers Bob and Tony Lockey, who became established in the mid-1950s as dismantlers and dealers of ex-military vehicles from a former brick works on the edge of a quarry high on the moors at Bingley. After adopting the title Bingley Autospares in 1963, they added the scrapping of passenger-carrying vehicles to their portfolio. Over the next twenty years, they dismantled a large number of buses and trolleybuses, the remains of which were dumped in the quarry. Due to persistent flooding, the quarry was filled with thousands of tonnes of rubble and soil in the late 1980s, burying the remains of its content, after which the company returned to its origins – military vehicles, cars and light commercials.

As stated earlier, in addition to its main activity as a dealer, W. North also scrapped a small number of buses itself at Stourton, as well as selling them to other breakers such as Bolland, Benny Johnson, Parker, Wigley and PVS. Of these, Wakefield-based Bolland also scrapped buses and lorries purchased directly from their operators and continued in business until the mid-1960s. Benny Johnson meanwhile, a nomadic person, joined the fray in 1966 and frequently moved premises (which largely comprised muddy pieces of waste land) – first around South Elmsall and then at Goldthorpe (often following altercations with the local council), taking with him on each occasion the caravan in which he lived. Then, after briefly moving to Carlton, he ceased his activities in the latter months of 1970 due to failing health.

Prior to this, Danny Parker, who for many years had been a collection/delivery driver for W. North, took the decision to work for himself. He rented a small plot of land behind a derelict textile mill on Musselburgh Street, Bradford, and in 1963 began to purchase a few buses from his former employer. However, prevented from growth by the size of his yard, he conceded defeat in 1972 and returned to his former occupation. Although W. North sold most of its unresaleable buses and coaches to the aforementioned breakers, in 1982 it gained a contract from London Transport to dismantle fifty-one Routemasters – the mechanical units from which were to be returned to London. In the event, however, it only broke up fifty at its Sherburn-in-Elmet premises, with the remaining example (RM1771) being hidden away, complete, before being resold several years later for further use.

Back in the Leeds area another firm entering the breaking industry was Colbro Ltd, who also traded as Diesel Engine Exporters from premises at Jawbone Works, Rothwell, which was only a mile or so away from W. North's yard at Stourton. Formed in 1955 by George Corson, Colbro almost immediately entered into an alliance with second-hand bus and coach dealer PVD at Woolston Grange, Rugby – a company set up by Harry Bowen who had previously worked for old established dealer Frank Cowley at Salford. In addition to scrapping diesel-powered buses (most of the engines of which were then exported), Colbro also dismantled a large number of ex-Bournemouth, Newcastle and Nottingham trolleybuses, selling their electrical components to operators overseas. Colbro continued until the latter years of the 1960s, when it ceased trading.

Further south in the Barnsley area was Wombwell Diesels, which began its bus breaking activities in 1959 as Chris Hoyle & Sons Ltd (previously general scrap dealers) from a former brick works at Station Road, Wombwell. Over the next few years the business developed dramatically, and after being renamed Wombwell Diesels Co. Ltd in 1965, it gained a contract from London Transport to dismantle forty RT-type AEC Regent double-deckers. From this small acorn the London Transport element of its business grew to the extent that around 4,000 buses from the capital met their end at Wombwell, including RTs, RTLs, RFs, AEC Merlins and Swifts, as did a large number of former NBC, PTE and municipal buses and coaches. In addition to its breaking activities, Wombwell Diesels also hired a few of its acquisitions to various operators before these too ultimately met their fate. After Chris and Wilf Hoyle decided to retire and close the business, they auctioned the remaining vehicles that were awaiting scrapping on 2 March 1994, with most being purchased by other Barnsley-area breakers.

Although Clarence Frederick Booth had begun as a general scrap merchant at Armer Street, Rotherham, in 1920, it was not until the early 1970s – by which time the company had expanded to be a major ferrous and non-ferrous metal recycler – that it turned its attention towards buses, railway locomotives and rolling stock. At first the buses acquired were from London Transport, but these were quickly followed by vehicles from a number of NBC companies as well as from PTEs and municipal fleets. While the majority of these were scrapped at Booth's Clarence Metal Works in Rotherham, a few were dismantled at Aston where, in the late 1970s, the company had acquired a site off Ulley Lane. In the mid-1980s, however, C. F. Booth left the PVS scrappage market to allow greater concentration on its railway and other aspects of its business, but surprisingly returned in 2017, when it scrapped a number of former London bendibuses.

To the east of Rotherham is Doncaster, and it was here that R. E. Trem & Co. began scrapping buses at its yards at Finningley and Woodsetts in 1961, continuing thus for around five years. Then came Barry Jameson, who entered the field on a muddy site at Dunscroft in 1973 before adopting the trading name Dunscroft Commercials in 1976. Three years later, however, Jameson left the industry and rented out his muddy site to E. Beckett, who since 1976 had been scrapping buses at Boulder Bridge Lane, Carlton, to where he returned in July 1980, after which Jameson recommenced his activities, first under the title PV Sales & Spares and then as Doncaster Bus Breakers. Although he scrapped numerous buses at his Dunscroft site, he also resold a great many to the Carlton breakers – and particularly PVS – for their final destruction.

By the mid-1950s Barnsley and its surrounds had become the major UK hub for bus and coach dismantling, with a number of different companies (and characters) becoming involved. Among the first was Allan Finlay, who began breaking buses on a small plot of land at Blacker Hill railway sidings in 1956. In 1963 he was joined by J. W. Swift, with whom he formed a partnership, although this lasted for less than a year before they each decided to go their separate ways; Finlay remained at Blacker Hill, while Swift moved to a small yard at Stairfoot. Two years later Finlay relocated to Birdwell, where he gained a new site that included some buildings in which he could store his stock of spares, and so on. Having now begun to trade as Hartwood Exports (Machinery) Ltd, he began exporting engines and other mechanical components as well as complete buses to numerous overseas countries. As his business expanded, he sought additional premises and took over a yard at Worsborough Dale which had been previously occupied by Paul Sykes. In addition, Finlay gained a third yard at Hoyland, but after removing all the mechanical units from the buses he acquired, he sold them to various Carlton breakers, including Paul Sykes, for their final destruction. In 1984, however, he took the decision to retire and closed the business, never to return.

In the meantime, Frank Thornton had entered the industry at Stairfoot in 1956, dismantling a number of buses on behalf of Wombwell Diesels, as well as a few he purchased independently. Three years later, Dennis Higgs began scrapping buses at Monk Bretton, buying most of his stock from THC and BET subsidiaries as well as from several municipal undertakings. However, after taking the decision to diversify into heavy plant hire, in February 1977 he leased part of his Monk Bretton premises to newcomers Dickinson & Shippey, who dismantled a small number of buses there until December 1978, when they too took the decision to leave the scrap industry. Upon their departure, however, yet another new breaker, Geoff Ripley, took over the lease and remained at Monk Bretton until July 1982, at which point he relocated to Boulder Bridge Lane, Carlton. Following this, Dennis Higgs surprisingly began to dismantle buses again, albeit only for two years before ceasing once more – this time not to return.

As the 1960s began to unfold, several more newcomers entered the bus breaking industry around Barnsley, one of whom was Ronald Askin, who acquired a plot of land behind Yorkshire Traction's depot on Upper Sheffield Road, not far from the town centre. Here, a large number of buses met their fate, with Ronald's son Ken taking over the business in 1976 and continuing it for a further eight years before ceasing his activities to pursue other business interests. Meanwhile, the industry continued to grow, with H. Evans starting to scrap buses at Worsborough Dale in 1965, but ceasing in less than a year, and Brian Laverack and Arnold Pickersgill forming a partnership and commencing their activities on a small plot of land at South Elmsall, some 10 miles from Barnsley. Then there was the previously mentioned Paul Sykes who, after working as a tyre fitter and small-time dealer in car parts, took the decision to enter the field of bus breaking and purchased his first 'scrapper' in 1961, which he broke up at Blacker Hill sidings. Purchasing his second bus from the proceeds of the first one, he soon had sufficient capital to buy more than one vehicle at a time and in 1967 he set up a business under the title of Dovecliffe Commercials at Worsborough Dale, Barnsley. This was associated with Hartwood Exports, to whom it was passed in 1969. By this time Paul Sykes had obtained several other small sites in the Barnsley area, although he continued to use Blacker Hill as his main yard, where he also scrapped numerous buses on behalf of Hartwood Exports. A few years later he diversified into dealing rather than breaking and rented his Blacker Hill site to his cousin Joe, who was just entering the bus dismantling industry.

The success of these new breakers encouraged more to enter the scene during the first part of the 1960s, with C. Meynell and Malcolm Parton forming a partnership and Milleon joining the fray, followed by L. Nutton in 1963, who based himself in Stairfoot, and Thomas Hardwick and George Jones, who set up as partners at Carlton. Growth continued rapidly, with Arthur Barraclough starting up in business at Shaw Lane, Carlton, in 1965 and Wilfred Conway and D. Dale forming a partnership that, in the event, lasted for less than a year, after which Conway diversified into car breaking under the title of Carlton Commercials. Following quickly on their heels was Fred Smith, who after trading by himself entered into a partnership with Tom Goodwin in 1968, as well as B. Fisher and Jim Ford, who set up in partnership at around the same time. Finally, before the decade ended, David Rollinson also took up the challenge.

By now, however, after encountering numerous difficulties with the local councils following complaints from residents living close to the breaker's yards at South

Elmsall, Goldthorpe, Blacker Hill and other localities around Barnsley, a decision was taken by those occupying these sites to move away as soon as a new location could be found. Upon hearing of a large area of derelict land at Boulder Bridge Lane, Carlton (which ran off Shaw Lane, where some breaking activity was already taking place), an approach for its use was quickly made, and after acceptance several bus dismantlers were able to relocate their businesses. Due to a railway embankment running along the back of the new site and the lack of drainage, the area was, unfortunately, almost permanently waterlogged.

Among Boulder Bridge Lane's first residents were Pickersgill & Laverack; Goodwin & Smith; Rollinson; Meynell; and Fisher & Ford, although it was not long before they were joined by newcomer Malcolm Parton, who had severed his partnership with Meynell and had formed a new one in 1972 with Allen. Although Pickersgill and Laverack continued in partnership until 1979 (when Pickersgill sold his share of the business to his partner and left the industry to become a coal merchant), they had also traded independently, with Brian Laverack adopting the title Passenger Vehicle Spares (Barnsley) Ltd (better known as PVS) in June 1972. During the early 1980s, PVS became the most prominent of the bus breakers at Boulder Bridge Lane, and after gaining the contract to dismantle all buses surplus to the requirements of APT (the NBC's Eastern Region disposal pool at Lincoln), it enjoyed similar arrangements with London Transport and Purfleet dealer Ensign.

In the meantime, another breaker to gain a site at Boulder Bridge Lane was James Whiting, who moved from South Elmsall in 1971 and also had a yard at Knottingley. Over the next few years a number of other breakers took plots on Boulder Bridge Lane, although most departed after only a few months, perhaps finding that dismantling buses was not as lucrative as they had first thought. There were a few, however, who stood the test of time a little better, albeit after disentangling themselves from previous partnerships or forming new ones. Among these was Eddie Hardwick, who ended his partnership with George Jones in 1976. Both continued independently, with Jones trading under the title Carlton Metals while Beckett joined forces with Meynell and moved to Boulder Bridge Lane from Pontefract, where he had started his activities in 1958. This new partnership proved to be brief, and in 1979 Beckett relocated to Dunscroft, where he rented the site previously used by Jameson. Two years later he returned to Boulder Bridge Lane when he entered into a partnership with James Sefton, although this only lasted for a few months, after which he continued on his own again at Pontefract. Meanwhile, following the untimely death of Fred Smith in 1974, Tom Goodwin continued in his own right, and from 1976 became the main breaker of time-expired buses no longer required by Middlewich-based bus and coach dealer Martins.

Yet another newbie to establish himself on Boulder Bridge Lane was Trevor Wigley, who in 1975 had set up in partnership with Frank Wells at Goldthorpe. This, however, only lasted briefly due to a disagreement as to the direction the business should proceed, and thus after working for relative Brian Laverack at PVS for a short while, Wigley set up his own business further along the Lane in 1977. Not surprisingly the two companies closely cooperated with each other until Trevor's untimely death in

2007, and in addition to forming a joint bus and coach sales operation, large batches of vehicles purchased by PVS for dismantling were often shared between them.

Following Wigley's debut, Geoff Ripley relocated from Monk Bretton to Boulder Bridge Lane in 1978. During the following year, Joe Sykes moved here from Blacker Hill when he took up residency of the premises previously occupied by E. Beckett until his departure back to Pontefract, where he concentrated largely on car dismantling, passing any buses he subsequently acquired to PVS for scrapping. In 1996 Joe Sykes took the decision to leave the industry and sold his yard and workshop to Alan Hardwick, who had traded as AJS Salvage since entering the industry in partnership with J. S. Linford in 1984. After ending their partnership in 1988, Hardwick had continued to trade independently from a site further along Boulder Bridge Lane, and had ultimately discontinued his AJS trading title. In more recent times, however, he has rented part of his large yard to a television catering company and a haulage contractor, although he still continues his bus breaking activities on what remains of his site.

Having reached its peak, the number of breakers located on Boulder Bridge Lane began to diminish during the 1990s, largely as a result of the increasing environmental regulations thrust upon them, some of which they found too expensive to undertake. David Rollinson was among the first to leave and departed in 1993, while soon afterwards Whiting Bros relocated to a site in the shadow of Ferrybridge power station, continuing their activities until April 1999, when, after taking the decision to retire, they sold all their remaining stock to PVS for scrapping. Then, after constantly flouting the new regulations and being given the ultimatum of 'comply or cease trading', Tom Goodwin, who also owned a farm and a retail decorative coverings shop, decided on the latter, and ceased trading in the summer of 2007.

Today, the only bus breakers remaining in the Barnsley area are Hardwick, Parton, PVS, Ripley and Wigley, all of whom continue to be located on Boulder Bridge Lane at Carlton after having largely met current environmental regulations and upgraded their premises.

This poor-quality photograph shows ex-Coventry City Transport, Brush-bodied Daimler CVD6 GKV 101, which has been cut down for use as a scrap carrier by Blamires, Bradford, in whose yard it is seen in 1965. Alongside are former Brighton & Hove, ECW-bodied Bristol K5Gs 412/0 (EPM 9/7).

Awaiting dismantling in Blamires' Bradford yard in the early 1960s are two ex-Newcastle Corporation, Roe-bodied Daimler CVG6s, a former Hull Corporation Sunbeam W trolleybus and an ex-London Transport AEC Q-type single-decker. (Author's collection)

Having been stored by Samuel Ledgard on the roof of its Armley depot since its withdrawal in 1943, Leyland TS1 UB5 740, with a body built by its operator, is seen here awaiting its fate at G. W. Butler's Bradford yard in July 1952. (Author's collection)

After spending twenty-four years stored on the roof of Ledgard's Armley depot, solid-tyred 1914 vintage Karrier charabanc U-2706 awaits its destruction at G. W. Butler's Bradford premises in June 1952. (Author's collection)

After spending ten years as Ledgard's Otley depot towing vehicle, 1928 Leyland PLSC3 KW4 581, which was new to B&B Tours, Bradford, is seen here in 1953 at G. W. Butler's Eller Ghyll yard, where it was ultimately scrapped. (Author's collection)

Standing together with some unidentified buses at Bingley Autospares on 21 December 1966 is former Newcastle Corporation, MCCW-bodied BUT 9641T trolleybus NBB 623. (Andy Feather)

New to Southdown, and previously used as a canteen by Manchester Corporation Direct Works, was this Park Royal-bodied Leyland PD1, which is seen at Bingley Autospares in October 1986.

Visible in Bingley Autospares' quarry in 1983 are a number of ex-military Bedford buses, while in the distance are several ex-Halifax Corporation and Bradford City Transport MCCW-bodied AEC Regent Vs, among other vehicles. (Andy Feather)

Being collected from W. North, Sherburn-in-Elmet, by Bradford-based breaker Danny Parker is ex-Farsley Omnibus Co. Roe-rebodied Daimler CVD6 KUM 849. It began life with Wallace Arnold, Leeds, in 1947 as a Wilks & Mead-bodied coach and was given its new double-deck body in 1957.

Soon to leave W. North's Stourton yard for Bolland's, Wakefield, where it would be scrapped in October 1961, is ex-West Yorkshire Road Car Co. ECW-bodied Bristol L5G SG62 (DWW 576). (Author's collection)

Ex-Midland General Weymann-bodied AEC Regent IIs 124/62 (KRB 74/9) stand alongside former Leeds City Transport, Roe-bodied AEC Regent III 408 (JUG 641) at Colbro, Rothwell, in March 1964. (Author's collection)

Colbro's yard at Jawbone Works, Rothwell, is seen here filled with ex-Newcastle and Nottingham Corporation trolleybuses on 29 December 1965. (Andy Feather)

Awaiting collection by a Carlton breaker from W. North's Sherburn-in-Elmet yard in July 1974 are four ex-West Yorkshire Bristol Lodekkas: FS6B 1692 (2226 WW) and LD6Bs DX81/66/17 (YWW 76, TWY 608 and OWX 161). (Author's collection)

Lined up outside W. North's Sherburn-in-Elmet premises, ready for collection by a Carlton breaker, in September 1974 are three AEC Reliances: ex-South Wales Weymann-bodied 216 (VWN 11), and two ex-Yorkshire Woollen District examples – Marshall-bodied 129 (GHD 760) and Park Royal-bodied 128 (FHD 128).

A trio of ex-Greater Glasgow PTE MCW Metropolitans, including M18 (GGA 72N) and M36 (JUS 756N), await their demise at W. North's Sherburn-in-Elmet premises in June 1982.

Seen being dismantled by W. North at its Sherburn-in-Elmet premises in 1984 is one of the fifty-one Routemasters acquired from London Transport during the previous year.

Having been used by the National Coal Board during the miners' strike and with steel grilles over all its windows is a former Bristol Omnibus Co. ECW-bodied Bristol LH6L, which is seen in W. North's Sherburn-in-Elmet yard in February 1985.

Seen outside W. North's Sherburn-in-Elmet premises, awaiting collection by a Carlton breaker, in October 1987 are the remains of three ex-South Yorkshire PTE Volvo Ailsa B55s, including 417 (NAK 417R) and 370 (LWB 370P), together with former Tyne & Wear PTE MCW Metropolitan 469 (RCU 469S).

Ex-Barton, Plaxton-bodied Leyland Leopard 1373 (OAL 617M), former Bee Line, ECW-bodied Bristol VRT 513 (MPM 391P) and ex-Teesside Motor Services ECW-bodied Bristol LH6L XEL 836K are seen near the end of their lives at W. North's Sherburn-in-Elmet yard in the latter months of 1990.

Standing in the gateway of Wombwell Diesels' premises for more than six years, where it is seen here in 1974, was former Southport Corporation English Electric-bodied Leyland TD3 145 (AFY 973), the top deck of which had been removed by its previous owner, Southport Sea Scouts. (Author's collection)

Seen at Wombwell Diesels in 1979 are seven ex-London RT-type AEC Regents. RT3254 (LLU 613) managed to escape the breaker's torch and was sold for preservation. (Barry Newsome)

Used internally in the yard of Wombwell Diesels as a scrap carrier/tow bus in 1979 is an unidentified ex-London Transport RT. The partly dismantled RT563 (HLX 380) can be seen in the background. (Author's collection)

After their bodies had been removed, the chassis of a number of ex-London Transport RTs await their ultimate demise at Wombwell Diesels in 1979.

Awaiting their fate at Wombwell Diesels in July 1981 are ex-Leeds City Transport Roe-bodied Leyland PDR2/1 369 (PNW 369G) and two ex-London Transport buses, RT1550 (KGU 442) and RF454 (MXX 431), both of which had spent time with other owners since leaving the capital.

Being broken up by C. F. Booth at its Aston site on 11 April 1981 are ex-Yorkshire Rider Daimler CRG6s: Alexander-bodied LAK 335G, which was new to Bradford City Transport, and Roe-bodied OCX 491F, which began life with Huddersfield Corporation. (Adrian Griffith)

Being collected by C. F. Booth on 15 April 1982 from the Spath depot of Stevenson (who had never operated it) is former Western SMT Alexander-bodied Albion Lowlander VCS 432.

Flanked by an ex-London AEC Swift and a former Greater Manchester PTE AEC Renown, two ex-PMT Leyland Atlanteans take centre stage together with an unidentified single-decker at Booth's Rotherham yard. (Adrian Griffith)

Starting life with Tayside Regional Council, and then passing through a number of owners, the last of whom was Brandon, Blackmore End, before ending its days in Jameson's Dunscroft yard in March 2000, is Alexander-bodied Bristol VRT OSR 194R, which is seen here alongside a former MoD single-decker.

Ex-Leon, Finningley MCW-bodied Leyland FE30AGR NOC 435R, which was new to West Midlands PTE, awaits its fate at Jameson's Dunscroft premises in March 2000. Alongside is NCME-bodied Daimler CRG6LXB GND 492N, which originated with Greater Manchester PTE.

Awaiting their ultimate fate outside Allan Finlay's Hartwood Diesels premises at Birdwell, Barnsley, in October 1974 are a trio of ex-Edinburgh Corporation MCCW-bodied Leyland PD2s, all of which would soon be scrapped for their engines and other mechanical units.

Lined up ready for dismantling at the Dennis Higgs Monk Bretton yard in 1964 are ex-Hants & Dorset Portsmouth Aviation-bodied Bristol L6G KEL64 and two ECW-bodied Bristol L5Gs: ex-York-West Yorkshire FWX 817 and former North Western CDB 189. (Author's collection)

Having already had their engines and front axles removed, ex-York-West Yorkshire ECW highbridge-bodied Bristol K6Bs YDB74 (HWW 885) and YDB71 (GWX 118) await scrapping at Dennis Higgs, Monk Bretton, in January 1963.

New to Darwen Corporation but later with Blackburn Corporation, East Lancs-bodied Leyland PD3A/1 MTJ 968C awaits its fate in August 1979 outside Dickinson & Shippey's Monk Bretton yard, which had previously been occupied by Dennis Higgs.

Looking through a wire fence into Askin's Barnsley yard, the contents of which include ex-NBC, BET and municipal buses from a variety of operators. (Thomas W. W. Knowles)

Two former Midland Red single-deckers are seen here at Askin's Barnsley yard in the process of being scrapped in the early 1980s.

Seen among the buses at Paul Sykes's Blacker Hill site are ex-Northern General Leyland Atlanteans, a former Bournemouth Leyland PD2 and an ex-Morecambe & Heysham open top AEC Regent III, some of which were scrapped on behalf of Hartwood Exports. (Barry Newsome collection)

An ex-Merseyside PTE Leyland PD2, a trio of former Greater Glasgow PTE Leyland Atlanteans and a pair of ex-Yorkshire Woollen District double-deckers take centre stage at the rural Blacker Hill yard of Paul Sykes. (Barry Newsome collection)

Two former South Yorkshire PTE Roe-bodied Daimler CVG6s – 1277 (CET 77C) and 1279 (DET 79C) – stand in the mud, partly dismantled, in the yard of Joe Sykes in March 1977. (Author's collection)

Being dismantled in Meynell's yard at Carlton in March 1984 is an unidentified ex-SELNEC NCME-bodied Daimler Fleetline.

Having just arrived at Rollinson's yard, former West Midlands PTE Park Royal-bodied Daimler CRG6LX 4269 (EOF 268L) is being unhooked from the wagon that has towed it from Birmingham.

First West Yorkshire has now disposed of all its Wright 'ftr'-bodied Volvo B7LAs to various breakers, with this example being shown in the yard of PVS, Carlton, in January 2018. (Author's collection)

New to Red & White and later serving with National Welsh and RHM Foods, Grantham, ECW-bodied Bristol RELL6G GAX 8C is seen here awaiting scrapping in Goodwin's muddy yard at Carlton in December 1985.

Among the buses tightly packed into Goodwin's yard at Carlton on 9 November 2000 are a Leyland National, an ECW-bodied double-decker, an ex-West Midlands PTE Fleetline and several ex-Arriva Merseyside, ex-London Leyland Titans.

Engineless and awaiting its fate at Goodwin's, Carlton, on 9 November 2000 is former Brylaine Alexander-bodied Leyland FE30AGR HSD 84V, as well as several ex-Arriva Merseyside Leyland Titans (including KYV 398/401X), and a former MTL Leyland Atlantean.

Standing in the typically deep mud in Goodwin's Carlton yard on 9 November 2000 are an Alexander-bodied Leyland Atlantean and a former London Leyland Titan, both of which had last been operated by Arriva Merseyside.

A trio from Stagecoach's Scottish fleet, Alexander-bodied Volvo B10M 20302 (L302 PSC), Northern Counties-bodied Leyland Olympian 16201 (L101 JSA) and an unidentified example, reach the end of their lives in Parton's Carlton yard in 2010. (Author's collection)

Seen in Parton's Carlton yard in August 2014 are ex-Cass, Moreton, Northern Counties-bodied Leyland Olympian C174 YBA and former HTL Buses, Huyton, Optare Solo V980 XUB.

New to Tyne & Wear PTE and latterly owned by Rapsons, Allness, Alexander-bodied Volvo Ailsa B55 GCN 3N is seen here in PVS's Boulder Bridge Lane yard in August 1991.

Former City Fleet, Liverpool, ECW-bodied Bristol VRT REH 813M awaits its destruction at PVS, Carlton, in May 1993, alongside three Routemasters – two ex-London and one ex-Clydeside/ Western Scottish.

Wedged between two Bristol VRTs and ex-Stevenson, Spath, Leyland Fleetline OUC 53R at PVS, Carlton, in June 1993 are two Routemasters – one ex-Clydeside, the other ex-London Buses – and two former South London Leyland Fleetlines, DMS 2421 and DMS 2335. (Barry Newsome)

Nearing its final destruction at PVS, Carlton, on 7 July 1995 is all that remains of a former Merseybus Leyland Atlantean.

Ex-Castle Point Bus Co. East Lancs-bodied Leyland PD3A/1 CJF 72C, an unidentified former Brighton & Hove Bristol VRT, former Appleby East Lancs-bodied Leyland FE30AGR NKU 563R and ex-North Western Park Royal-bodied Leyland AN68/1R PUF 721M await their fate at PVS, Carlton, in 1995.

Purchased by PVS at the Yorkshire Rider auction on 20 May 1996, ex-Quickstep Travel Leyland Nationals 10 (YWW 810S) and 51 (MEL 551P) are seen at its Boulder Bridge Lane yard later that year.

Seen at PVS, Carlton, in 1996 after being set alight and with its wheels removed is ex-Yorkshire Rider Dormobile-bodied Freight Rover Sherpa 1870 (D870 LWR).

Ex-London Leyland Titan T989 (A989 SYE) and an unidentified MCW Metrobus stand with former Luton & District, ex-Stuart Palmer/London Transport Leyland Fleetlines 964 (OJD 363R) and 965 (OJD 425R) in the Carlton yard of PVS in 1998.

Following its purchase of all the remaining stock of Ferrybridge breaker Whiting Bros upon its closure in April 1999, PVS's yard at Boulder Bridge Lane, Carlton, had insufficient unoccupied space to accommodate its new acquisitions, and as a consequence temporarily stored them at the adjacent WFS Metals site, which is where they are pictured.

Ex-Kelvin Central Buses Routemaster 1918 (EDS 395A, ex-WLT 538) and an unidentified former London Routemaster stand in PVS's Carlton yard in March 2000. Alongside is Ensign Enterprise Daimler CRG6 B56 DAR, which had been rebuilt in 1985 from London DMS 237.

Having previously been offered for sale by PVS at Cudworth, but failing to find a buyer, ex-Greater Glasgow PTE Alexander-bodied Leyland AN68 LA1370 (RDS5 49W) was moved to the Boulder Bridge Lane premises at Carlton, where it is seen standing alongside a former West Midlands Travel MCW Metrobus.

Two ex-First Bradford Leyland AN68s, an unidentified ex-Northern Bus ECW-bodied Bristol RELH and former Reading Mainline Routemaster 2 (WLT 993) await their ultimate fate at PVS, Carlton, in May 2001.

Former London Buses Routemaster RM14 (OYM 424A, ex-VLT 14) was originally preserved by PVS, Carlton, with whom it is seen in August 2001. It was sold to a private preservationist in February of the following year.

An aerial view of PVS's yard at Boulder Bridge Lane, Carlton, showing a wide variety of buses, including Bristol VRTs, Leyland Titans and a former London DMS Fleetline awaiting destruction. (PVS Ltd)

All that is left of a former Lesney Products ex-London RT stands alongside ex-East Yorkshire Roe-bodied Leyland Atlantean 872 (PRH 246G) in the yard of PVS, Carlton, in February 2008.

Piles of scrap bodywork tower above and surround the remains of an ex-First Group single-decker and three double-deckers at PVS, Carlton, on 26 January 2009.

New to Eastern Counties, but latterly preserved, ECW-bodied Bristol RELL6G IIL 2271 (ex-BVF 668J) stands alongside two Plaxton-bodied Dennis Lances – First West Yorkshire M435 VWW and an Arriva North West example – and a former First South Yorkshire Alexander-bodied Volvo B10M in PVS's Carlton yard on 11 November 2009.

New to London Buslines, but finally with First West Yorkshire, Northern Counties-bodied Leyland Olympian 31738 (H134 FLX), seen here at PVS, Carlton, on 19 January 2011, will survive for less than another hour before entering the annals of history.

Former First Manchester Wright-bodied Volvo B10BLE 21169 (R627 CVR) keeps company with five partly dismantled ex-First Leeds Wright-bodied Volvo B10LA bendibuses in the yard of PVS, Carlton, on 22 July 2013.

Having just arrived on tow from First Leeds on 22 July 2013, Alexander-bodied Volvo Olympian 30247 (S663 NUG) is hauled across the yard of PVS, Carlton, by a forklift truck to await its fate.

Four ex-First West Yorkshire buses are seen here at PVS, Carlton, in August 2014, several years after their arrival.

Having been a resident of PSV's Carlton yard for over two decades, former Top Deck Travel ECW-bodied Bristol FLF6G VCS 375, which was new to Western SMT, is seen being finally scrapped on 25 November 2016.

Displaying three different liveries, ex-Stagecoach Manchester Alexander-bodied Dennis Tridents 17245 (X371 NNO), 17641 (W641 RND) and 17271 (X271 NNO) await their fate at PVS, Carlton, on 25 November 2016.

After standing at the back of PVS's Carlton yard since February 2009, ex-Thamesdown Northern Counties-bodied Daimler CVG6 JAM 144E had been moved closer to the scrapping area by 15 March 2017.

Optare Solos are now starting to arrive in the yards of the Barnsley breakers, as illustrated by ex-First Bradford 53034 (Y546 XNW), which is seen here at PVS on 15 March 2017. Alongside are former West Midlands Travel MCW Metrobus 2685 (A685 UOE) and ex-First Bradford Alexander-bodied Volvo Olympian 30891 (W746 DWX).

Seen at PVS, Carlton, on 15 March 2017 are three roofs that have been removed from the heavily cannibalised Routemasters standing alongside. The roofs were awaiting transportation to their new owner, Lothian Buses, who had purchased six for possible transplanting onto their recently withdrawn open top sightseeing RMs.

With a lot number chalked on its front panel indicating that it had been purchased via an auction, a former Bassetts of Tittensor Foden coach awaits scrapping at Wigley's Carlton yard in November 1984.

Acquired by Wigley, Carlton, from Cardiff breaker W. A. Way was a former Cardiff trolleybus, which is seen here in November 1984 standing alongside ex-City of Oxford ECW-bodied Bristol RELH6G 73 (GBW 73L).

In the autumn of 1984, Wigley purchased a number of ex-CIE, Dublin, Leyland Atlanteans for scrapping – three of which are seen here at Carlton in November of that year.

Purchased from London by PVS, these Routemasters were passed to Wigley's for scrapping and are seen awaiting their fate in December 1984.

Latterly used as a driver trainer, rare Wadham Stringer-bodied Volvo B57-50 RMH 869Y stands in Wigley's Carlton yard in December 2000 alongside former Trent Leyland National 514 (ACH 514T), which is wearing Blue Apple livery.

After breaking down in the UK, this Romanian Roman coach ended its life in the yard of Wigley, Carlton.

Starting life with South Notts and ending it with Verwood Transport, Northern Counties-bodied Daimler CRL6 NNN 99K and ex-MR Travel Rochdale ECW-bodied Leyland Leopard YEL 92Y, which was new to Hants & Dorset, await their turn for scrapping at Wigley's, Carlton, in May 2001.

Ex-United Leyland National 2 3148 (ARN 896Y), which was new to Ribble, is seen here in Wigley's Carlton yard in August 2001 with the remains of a double-decker standing on its roof.

A month after being burnt out on the A1 at Great Casterton on 7 August 2005, Stagecoach East's Jonckheere-bodied Volvo B10M 52620 (S460 BCE) awaits its final demise at Wigley's, Carlton, later that year.

Partly scrapped ex-Arriva North East Optare MetroRider 880 (N880 RTN) stands alongside a pile of tangled metal in Wigley's Carlton yard on 18 September 2007.

Looking in pristine condition are ex-Lavender of Heanor's former Colchester Leyland Lynx H29 MJN and ex-Shamrock, Bournemouth's former Eastbourne Northern Counties-bodied Leyland Olympian 250 (E850 DPN). Both had only recently arrived at Wigley's, Carlton, when photographed on 18 November 2011.

New to London Buses but lastly owned by Square Peg, Garforth, Alexander-bodied Scania N113DRB J816 HMC awaits destruction along with several coaches and minibuses at Wigley's, Carlton, on 15 March 2017.

With smoke rising from the chassis being cut up, a variety of buses from several different operators are stacked on top of each other in Wigley's Carlton yard on 15 March 2017.

Still in Arriva livery, ex-MASS, Anston, Alexander-bodied DAF DB250 S281 JUA and former Stagecoach East Kent Alexander-bodied Dennis Trident 17690 (X602 VDY) stand alongside Neoplan Skyliner LUI 6247 (ex-F619 CWJ), which is partly buried under a huge pile of scrap, in Wigley's Carlton yard on 8 August 2017.

Two of the ex-Eastern Counties ECW highbridge-bodied Bristol Ks purchased by Ripley, Carlton, from East Anglian breaker Ben Jordan near their ultimate demise at Boulder Bridge Lane in November 1984.

One of several former Stockport all-Leyland PD2s acquired by Ripley of Carlton from the erstwhile Berresford of Cheddleton, DJA 186 is well on its way to disappearing into the annals of history while one of its sisters waits its turn in the background in August 1987.

Ripley's yard at Carlton with a variety of buses, including an ex-Hunt's of Alford Leyland National. (P. T. Stokes)

Originally London Country LNC24 (NPD 124L) and later purchased by East Yorkshire Motor Services, who re-registered it JKH 119L, this Leyland National was latterly used by Wallace Arnold of Leeds as an interchange control unit. It is seen here in Ripley's Carlton yard in November 2000.

A former Black Prince, Morley, MCW Metropolitan (OCU 782R) stands alongside an ex-Midway Leyland National at Ripley's, Carlton. (Barry Newsome)

Four ex-MASS, Anston, ex-London Leyland Titans stand in the Carlton yard of Ripley together with other buses, including D Coaches of Morriston's ex-GM Buses Northern Counties-bodied Leyland Atlantean 4604 (ANA 604Y). (Author's collection)

Goodwin of Carlton's former premises were used by Ripley as an overflow yard on 19 August 2014, where a former West Midlands Travel MCW Metrobus, an ex-London Mercedes-Benz 0530G bendibus and two former Arriva North West Mercedes-Benz bendibuses are among the vehicles temporarily stored there.

Standing in the yard of erstwhile breaker Goodwin, Carlton, before moving across the road into Ripley's premises on 8 August 2017 are ex-Stagecoach Merseyside Wright-bodied Scania L94UB driver trainer 28543 (Y962 XBO), former Keighley & District Alexander-bodied Volvo Olympian 989 (S59 VNM) and ex-First Cymru Marshall-bodied Dennis Dart SLF 41392 (X392 HLR).

Resting in Ripley's Carlton overflow yard on 8 August 2017 are ex-London Bus Company open-top Leyland Olympian J317 BSH, former Ultimate Coaches Plaxton-bodied Volvo B10M YIL 4067 and an ex-GHA, Ruabon, East Lancs-bodied Dennis Dart SLF.

Lined up at Hardwick's Carlton premises in 1995 are a Leyland Leopard converted to a towing wagon, ex-Andrews, Sheffield, MCCW-bodied AEC Regent V NNY 759E, which was sold for conversion to a traveller's home, former Dobson's Leyland National WWO 639T and ex-Age Concern Leyland National WNO 557L.

Awaiting scrapping at Hardwicks, Carlton, in February 2001 is Park Royal-bodied Daimler CRL6 TGX 806M, which started life with London Transport and ended it as a promotional vehicle for Charly Records.

Having already lost its engine, ex-Stagecoach Midland Red Alexander-bodied Leyland Fleetline DCU 819R stands alongside Leyland National BVP 771V from the same operator at Hardwick's, Carlton, in May 2001.

A former First Midland Red Mercedes-Benz 709D stands together with ex-Merseyside Travel, Liverpool, Northern Counties-bodied Dennis Dominator B902 TVR in Hardwick's Carlton yard in May 2007.

Awaiting scrapping at Hardwick, Carlton, in August 2014 are, among others, four double-deckers from Scottish independent Davies, Plean, and an ex-Arriva single-decker.

Although ex-Arriva buses dominate Hardwick's Carlton yard in November 2016, some buses from Stagecoach are also visible, as too is one from National Express West Midlands.

Former Tyne & Wear PTE MCW Metropolitan 450 (OTN 450R) stands alongside an ex-London Country Leyland Atlantean in Whiting's Ferrybridge yard.

Tucked into Whiting Bros' cramped yard at Ferrybridge in March 1999 a few weeks before its closure upon its owner's retirement are an ex-West Midlands Travel MCW Metrobus and Village Tours Alexander-bodied V32 (ASD 29T), which began life with A1 Service, Ardrossan.

Standing in Whiting Bros' yard in the shadows of Ferrybridge power station's cooling towers in March 1999 are ex-Merseybus Alexander-bodied Leyland Atlantean 1939 (ACM 739X), former Kentish Bus PMT-bodied Freight Rover Sherpa D179 CRE, an unidentified ex-Classic, Annfield Plain, double-decker and ex-Fareway, Liverpool, NCME-bodied Daimler CRG6 YNA 352M.

Collection and Dismantling

Both the collection of vehicles and the methods used for their dismantling have changed dramatically over the years and no longer is the sledge hammer the only tool of destruction. Initially, scrapping a bus was a long and physically demanding process, with little in the form of mechanisation to assist, whereas today it is customary for a bus to be reduced from a complete vehicle to a pile of twisted metal in less than thirty minutes with the use of a massive hydraulic claw-fingered grab and electromagnets. No longer can seat cushions, rubber, painted or treated wood or tyres be legally burned. All now have to be collected for off-site disposal, which is costing the larger breakers up to £1,000 per week. As time moved on and regulations increased, the yards could no longer be protected by flimsy boundary fencing. Instead, they now have to have substantial walls, all surfaces to be impermeable, to have a sealed drainage system, and to have appropriate storage areas and containers for batteries and parts containing oil. Each site has to be licensed by the Environmental Agency, have a nominated Technical Components Manager and comply with Defra's 'Depolluting End of Life Vehicles' regulations. In addition to all of this, all rubber, plastics, wire, brake linings and spring hangers (which are made from a different type of steel) have to be removed from a vehicle before weighing it in as scrap steel or aluminium, and thus it is of paramount importance that careful sorting is carried out in order to obtain the best prices from metal factors. Unlike the old days when it was customary to use guard dogs to protect their premises, all the breakers now have CCTV cameras located around their yards for this purpose, as well as having walls topped with razor wire to prevent trespassers and thieves from gaining access.

In addition to the changes that have taken place in respect of the actual dismantling process, the method of collecting vehicles purchased for scrapping has also changed dramatically. Initially vehicles were driven on trade plates under their own power to the site of their ultimate destruction whenever possible, while those that needed towing were hauled by lightweight wagons such as Ford Thames, Bedfords or Commers, etc. It was also the norm rather than the exception for some of their previously purchased buses to be cut down for use as towing vehicles – usually double-deckers whose upper body parts and rear platform had been removed – until they became mechanically unfit and were then scrapped. Now, however, legislation has gradually forced the industry to use more specialised towing vehicles, and to this end a number of the Carlton breakers began to construct their own wagons. Their preferred method was to acquire a short-wheelbase artic unit, chop it in two, lengthen the chassis by around 4 feet and then build specialist lifting gear onto it, usually a large RSJ with a swan neck for the actual lift. By attaching an A-frame to the vehicle to be towed and removing its front wheels it then virtually became a two-wheeled trailer, although this was not always the case and some buses were instead suspended towed. However, with the increasing cost of fuel and wages, new methods of collection were sought, and to this end PVS purchased a MAN TGA26 430 tractor unit in 2011, which is capable of carrying a full-length single-deck bus on its two-axle trailer and towing another full-length bus behind. This enables two vehicles to be collected at the same time, greatly reducing costs.

The purchasing of buses and coaches by those involved in the dismantling industry is not as straightforward as many might think as most of the larger bus and coach operators now invite tenders for their redundant vehicles rather than put a price tag on them. Therefore, it is necessary to take numerous variables into account when tender prices are calculated – not least the current prices being paid by metal factors for steel, aluminium and copper etc., all of which are extremely volatile and subject to frequent change. As a consequence, knowledge of vehicle types is essential – i.e. the amount of various metals that can be retrieved from for example a Leyland National or a Dennis Dart; the cost of materials needed to undertake the dismantling process; the completeness and condition of the bus in question; and the cost of removal of non-recyclable residue. Added to all of this is the distance that must be travelled to collect the vehicle, and as a result of all the above the prices offered can vary considerably from week to week.

Looking at the Boulder Bridge Lane occupants alone, PVS is able to break up to three buses per day, which equates to around 750 buses per year, and it can thus be said that the company has been responsible for the demise of over 15,000 vehicles over the last quarter of a century. Wigley's total is only slightly less, while Ripley & Hardwick scrap around 500 buses each year, and Parton only around 150.

This, then, is the story of the bus dealing and breaking industry in Yorkshire from its foundations to the present day, with Carlton ultimately becoming the hub of this form of activity within the county. Enthusiasts must be warned, however, that they will not be permitted to enter any of the yards on Boulder Bridge Lane and that should they attempt to gain access illegally they will be seen on CCTV and either prosecuted or dealt with in the old established 'Barnsley manner'. Need one say more?

The massive claws of PVS's grab tear off more of the Alexander bodywork of ex-Stagecoach East Midlands Volvo Olympian 16469 (S169 RET) on 15 March 2017, while former First West Yorkshire's similar combination 30805 (R625 JUB) stands alongside, knowing that it will be its turn next.

Resting at Scratchwood Services on the M1 motorway en route to dealer W. North, Sherburn-in-Elmet, on 9 January 1973 are ex-Hants & Dorset ECW-bodied Bristol K6Bs KEL 702, which is being driven on trade plates under its own power, and KEL 705, which is being towed.

Heading to a Carlton breaker on behalf of Hartwood Exports on 4 July 1968, and hauled by former Birmingham Corporation all-Leyland PD2 JOJ 154, which had been cut down to a tow truck, is ex-Darwen Corporation all-Crossley DD42/7 35 KTD 371.

With roles reversed, after failing en route to Yorkshire, Wombwell Diesels' ex-Southdown all-Leyland PD2/1 JCD 92, which had been cut down to a towing wagon, is being towed along the M1 motorway on 30 May 1969 by the bus it had been sent to collect, ex-London Transport RTL1392 (MXX 102).

Cut down to a towing wagon and scrap-carrier by C. F. Booth, Rotherham, is ex-Greater Manchester PTE MCCW-bodied Leyland PD2/40 FRJ 239D, which began life with Salford City Transport. (Adrian Griffith)

Being towed through Carlton village on its way to PVS's Boulder Bridge Lane yard on 21 August 2001 is former First Manchester Northern Counties-bodied Leyland Atlantean A738 NNA.

Arriving at PVS's Carlton yard on tow from Grant Palmer, Luton, on 20 December 2005 is Alexander-bodied Leyland Atlantean GSC 641X, which is still wearing the livery of its original owner, Lothian Buses.

A big wagon to tow a little bus! Having just arrived at Wigley's Carlton premises after being hauled from First Cymru on 9 May 2007 is Plaxton-bodied Mercedes-Benz 709D 51221 (M221 VWU), which started life with First West Yorkshire.

Purchased new by PVS of Carlton, this MAN wagon (PVS 1 W) was built specially to enable one bus to be carried on its platform and to simultaneously suspended tow another one behind. (PVS Ltd)

Towed by Whiting Bros' ERF wagon (HWX 402Y), an ex-London Country, former GM Buses Leyland Atlantean arrives at its new owner's Ferrybridge premises in April 1993.